بالقلم

# BY THE PEN

Ibrahim Muhammad Heshaam Jaaber

Written By: Ibrahim Muhammad Heshaam Jaaber

Copyright 2014 by Ibrahim Muhammad Heshaam Jaaber

First Edition, 2014


Published by Color Me Muslim LLC

P.O. Box 189, Roselle NJ

ColorMeMuslim@gmail.com

www.colormemuslim.us

Published first in the United States of America

# BY THE PEN

# BIOGRAPHY

Ibrahim Muhammad Heshaam Jaaber is a third generation American born Muslim, and the President and Founder of Color Me Muslim LLC which is an organization dedicated to social and cultural advancement in the Muslim community. At an early age, Ibrahim began to recognize certain obstacles and challenges that the Muslim communities and the youth in particular faced as regards to how this perfected way of life should translate into our everyday affairs. It became apparent to him that there were areas within the Islamic dynamic that had not yet taken shape in the secular world which consequently led some Muslims to search elsewhere for that fulfillment that Islam in it's true application would provide.

After many years struggling to find his niche within the Islamic movement, he finally realized that it was up to the Muslim youth to carve out something for themselves. It was then that his journey as a writer, spoken word poet and performer begin to unfold. However, as Allah would have it, Ibrahim was also becoming a very talented young basketball player as well and so consequently, for much of his life he was walking a double path. His days were consumed with basketball and his nights were consumed with poetry and although he would get the opportunity while in college to perform with one of the most renowned spoken word groups in the United States, his reputation on the basketball court completely overshadowed his reputation as an artist. In fact his ability would take him all the way to the pros where he got the opportunity to play at the highest level-even knocking on the door of the NBA on more than one occasion.

Now that Ibrahim has left basketball behind he has rekindled his passion for poetry and set out to use his experience to benefit the Muslim communities in whatever way possible. It has been nearly fifteen years since he begin his journey as a writer and the time has finally come for him to share his vision with the world.

# FORWARD

We begin with The Name of Allah, The Ever Merciful, The Especially Merciful. All praise belongs to Allah and to Allah alone. Therefore, we praise Him, we seek His assistance, we ask for His forgiveness, and we place all of our faith in Him alone as well as our trust. I send Salutations upon His beloved Prophet and Messenger Muhammad (SAW) who was sent as a bringer of good news, an open and plain warner, and a bright and shining star who called to Allah by His permission.

Thereafter, I would like to thank my family for the continuous support that they have been throughout my life. I treasure you all because you are a gift from Allah and for the same reason I honor and respect you. When Allah put us together it was by divine wisdom and as life continues to unfold I am able to experience that wisdom and understand it just a little bit more. May Allah continue to bless the family and guide us all to the straight path and allow us to reunite one day in the highest level of paradise. Ameen!

I would also like to blow a kiss to my wife and two young children who sacrifice every day in time and in energy in order to support me and my vision. Not only do you light up my house but the joy that you give off is inspiration for me to strive to bring forth my very best. May Allah reward you all with goodness and elevate your ranks with everyday that He allows us to share. Ameen!

Lastly, I pray that Allah puts His blessing upon this project and except it on my scale of good deeds, and make it a source of inspiration for muslims far and wide. It is not without His guidance and His mercy and His favor that I could have been able to produce the poems that fill the pages of this book and so to him is the true dedication of all good as we are commanded:

قُلْ إِنَّ صَلَاتِي وَنُسُكِي وَمَحْيَايَ وَمَمَاتِي لِلَّهِ رَبِّ الْعَالَمِينَ

SAY! INDEED MY PRAYER, MY SACRIFICE, MY LIFE AND MY DEATH ARE ALL FOR ALLAH THE LORD OF ALL THAT EXIST. [Quran 6 : 162]

5

# INTRODUCTION

Allah swears an oath in the Quran, when He says:

وَالْقَلَمِ وَمَا يَسْطُرُونَ

**BY THE PEN** AND ALL THAT THEY WRITE

[Quran 68 : 1]

In Islam The Pen bares great significance and is the ultimate symbol of Divine Decree as one of the narrations of the Prophet Muhammad (SAW) says, "As soon as Allah created The Pen, He commanded it to write. It said: "what should I write my Lord?" Allah said: "Write the record of all things that will happen until the establishment of The Hour" (Abu Dawud).

This is the reality that shapes the mentality of the muslim and it ultimately impacts the way he views this world. It provides insight to the circumstances of our lives, and gives meaning and color to the events of time. But too often we become disconnected from this reality, and we don't live in the consciousness of Divine Decree. But, whether we realize it or not, we are constantly witnessing it every moment that we exist.

It is not by coincidence that we have been made a nation who's first revelation was the commandment to "Read!" For reading the Quran teaches us how to read our lives. Reading the Quran, which contains the stories of real men and women and real events in time, expands our intellects and give us a deeper insight and understanding of Divine Decree. This should, in turn, produce enough wisdom within us to derive meaning from our own experiences for we are also real men and women, witnessing real events that also carry deep lessons that we can benefit from.

We are from what Allah has written.
We are from what Allah has decreed.
And life is not simply something that we live
it is also something that we can read.

By The Pen represents this deeper reality, a transcendent way of seeing the life that we lead- understanding that "INDEED, IT IS ALL IN A WRITTEN RECORD. SURELY THAT IS EASY FOR ALLAH" [Quran 22:70] It is with this consciousness that I bring forth this concept that splits the path that I walk everyday as both a Muslim and a Poet- pondering over the abstract and seeking to understand the deeper levels of life.

I do not intend to present an academic analysis of Divine Decree and it's tenants in regards to the Quran and Sunnah for that is a matter to be explained by the scholars of Islam, rather I intend to use poetry to capture it's reality as it has manifest in my life and my understanding of the world i.e. how one thing leads to the next, how certain things can not be prevented or avoided and how we all have a destiny that is unfolding before our very eyes. None of us knows the future- that is a right reserved for Allah alone, the only thing I can do is try to understand my life in the context of Divine Decree, to take the lessons and the insights that the Quran presents and use them to navigate this world. All I can do is refer back to Allah and His book for inspiration and guidance. In Him there is the knowledge and wisdom of all things and if ever we are able to understand the twist and the turns that life takes us on, then it will only be through Allah for He is the one who:

الَّذِي عَلَّمَ بِالْقَلَمِ    عَلَّمَ الْإِنسَانَ مَا لَمْ يَعْلَمْ

HE IS THE ONE WHO TAUGHT **BY THE PEN**
HE TAUGHT MAN THAT WHICH HE DID NOT KNOW
[Quran 80 : 4-5]

# COMMANDED TO READ

The decree of Allah is written
and I am commanded to read
And the book that I'll been handed
is the life that I'll lead

Allow me to wipe away the sleep
from the corner of my eyes
Collecting like dust on the cover
of an ancient text
How long have I been dreaming
When I should've been reading
Peeling back the pages
printed in the depths of my pupils
Attempting to peer through time-
and witness the visions
that were given to The Prophets

I listen to my eyes...
I listen with my eyes
to the wisdom of words
written on the distant surface
of the third dimension
Every story should start with a prayer

So I break like dawn-
the silence of chapters untold
marching through the morning cold
before Fajr unfolds,
just to arrive on time
for the Athan, the Iqama,
the opening verses of Quran,
from Takbeer to Salaam
Indulging in the essence of Islam

Submission-
doesn't always happen over night
Some people bare witness at birth
and don't achieve piety their entire life
Looking in the wrong direction-
when the compass for heaven
is seated in the chest
of those who believe
and the pin that spins within
already told us to read

But hearts that are in the dark
will not lead us to the Qibla
So we memorize the map-
we are the people of the scripture!

Read!
Resonates with the heaviest weight
pressing upon my chest plate
Read! Its the only way to breathe
Read! Until the pages bleed
Read! Echoes the struggles
of Allah's servants
over the surface of my retina

In the blink of an eye,
I see the ink drip, settle and dry
and the wing tips of angels cover the sky-
left man with the message
that will forever apply:
Remember the life of The Prophets
and revelation will never die

And never be mistaken
by the devil's reply
He'll look you dead in the eye
and tell you a lie
So don't follow his whispers
looking for passage
Hell is what you'll find
wrong side the fork in his tongue

Falling into Fitnah like a pit
in the folds of the forbidden
Picture: the vividest image of souls
fading away until forgotten
See your reflection as it darkens?
Nothing holy goes on outside the margins

Rather, righteousness is written
between the lines
in the shades of a radiant light
So let every day begin with prayer,
and blessed will be the stories
that fill the pages of your life...

The decree of Allah is written
and I am commanded to read
And the book that I'll been handed
is the life that I'll lead

اقْرَأْ بِاسْمِ رَبِّكَ الَّذِي خَلَقَ

READ! IN THE NAME OF YOUR LORD
WHO CREATED

خَلَقَ الْإِنسَانَ مِنْ عَلَقٍ

HE CREATED MANKIND FROM A CLOT

اقْرَأْ وَرَبُّكَ الْأَكْرَمُ

READ! AND YOUR LORD IS THE MOST GENEROUS

الَّذِي عَلَّمَ بِالْقَلَمِ

HE WHO TAUGHT BY THE PEN

عَلَّمَ الْإِنسَانَ مَا لَمْ يَعْلَمْ

HE TAUGHT MAN WHAT HE DID NOT KNOW

[QURAN 80 : 1-5]

# SCRIPTURE MY HOPES

I want to know Mecca to Medina by foot
but I'm too busy with life
I want to know Abraham like a father
and I'll be the sacrifice

I want to know Jerusalem like
the true followers of Christ
but Moses did not know The Promised Land
yet he was still granted paradise

I want to know what its like
to travel to heaven and back in one night
I want to know what it's like
to stand in the shadow of Adam's height

I want to know love, I want to know light
I want to know what it's like
to hear The Angels recite

I want to know The Book
as if it was written in my heart
I want to know what Noah felt
when he was building his Ark

I want to know moons that split
and seas that part
I want to know the waterways
upon which Jesus walked

I want to know sacred
before man set out to change it
I want to know the scriptures
in their original language

I want to know The Torah in hebrew
and The Gospels in aramaic
I want to hear The Psalms
in the voice of David

I want to know the prayer of Jonah
in the belly of the whale
I want to know the prayer of Joseph
in the bottom of the well

I want to know the prayer of John
when they locked him in a cell
I want to know what would've happened
if Adam never fell

I want to know heaven like home,
I want to know Solomon's throne
I want to know Goliath overthrown
and I'll be the stone!

And I don't want a crown I want a dome
and pillars made of chrome
I want faith to consume me
I want to feel it in my bones

I want the truth to be known,
I want the proof to be shown
until we wash away the blood of Athens
and the fingerprints of Rome

I want a moment of my own,
me and The Messengers alone
And how unbelievable it would be
just to recite them a poem

But see, my life is a pen
and so I've been writing all my wrongs
Reunited with the righteous,
it's like I'm right where I belong

I want to know the basket
that carried Moses up the nile
and the key that lifted the shackles
from the ankles of Bilal

I want to know what it's like
to be chosen above the crowd
and to overcome the trials
like Joseph as a child

I want to know Jacob (Ya'qub)
the father of a nation
Still not forgotten
for a thousand generations

I want to know Islam
without the innovations
I want my people to worship The Creator
and not the creation

I want to know Ali, young and courageous
Hamza and Umar some of the bravest
I want to know Abu Bakr
in The Battle of Badr
Usama bin Zaid- A warrior beyond age

And how many more that historians-
have torn from the page
Over 120,000 prophets
and we only know a few of their names

I want to know wisdom like Luqman
advising his son
I want to know purity
through the eyes of the young

I want to know victory
before my time here is done
I want to see this Ummah
UNITED AS ONE!

I want to know the straight path
like the back of my hand
Embody The Quran
like Muhammad- The map of a man

I want to nomad my way
across the desert like a shepherd
who's memorized every ancient path
known to The Fertile Crescent

I want to backpack Islam
from Giza to Gaza
on my don't look back
until I reach the Ka'ba

And many learn The Deen from scholars
but what if you had the opportunity
to sit at the feet of The Sahaba
..or better yet The Prophet
standing upon his minbar-
just before we break bread
with the companions at Iftar

I want to know my Creator -
that He is pleased with His slave
and I want Him to know that I am grateful
for all that He gave

I want to remember this world
through the eyes of faith
Just a stranger without a name
but many recognize the face
Standing upon a place
outside of time and space
I'm just a traveler in this world
trying to find my place

## The Prayer of Abraham

رَبِّ هَبْ لِي حُكْمًا وَأَلْحِقْنِي بِالصَّالِحِينَ
وَاجْعَل لِّي لِسَانَ صِدْقٍ فِي الْآخِرِينَ
وَاجْعَلْنِي مِن وَرَثَةِ جَنَّةِ النَّعِيمِ

My Lord! Grant me wisdom in judgement
and join me with the righteous!
And make for me an honorable mention
among latter generations!
And make me from the inheritors
of The Garden of Bliss!

[Quran 26 : 83-85]

# GREATER THAN STRIFE

Why do we approach the prayer
with hatred in our hearts,
worry on our minds
and hurry in our steps?
We need to let go of the burdens
that we carry in our chest-
like anchors made of anger
that weigh down our words
And yet we wonder why in the world
are our prayers not heard

But how can we worship Allah-
standing before Him
completely in awe
while the emotions inside
are completely at war?
We need to empty our hearts
of everything impure
and fill it up with Noor

Because we can never find peace
 until the stress is released
and that which is best
replaces that which is least

If this Dunya is on our mind
and we're worried about time
and we came to the prayer
while leaving nothing behind-
did we pray?
Did we pray- when everything else
is still standing in our way?

If we can't let go of this world
a few times everyday
then how much does our love
and our faith really weigh?
How much does our hope
and our fear really weigh?
How much does our speech really weigh
when our prayers contradict
the words that we say?

Allahu Akbar! on our tongues
yet our hearts remain numb
and the meaning escapes us
like the air from our lungs
But just because you breathe out phrases
of glory and praise,
bend your limbs and lower your gaze
doesn't mean that your mind and your heart

and your soul are engaged.
Thoughts wandering-
I've been wondering
are we just lost in a daze?
covering our darkness
in the cloth of a slave?
If we want to survive...

We have to let The Light of Allah inside-
to cast out the demons
that are haunting our lives
They tell us nothing but lies
to keep our minds occupied
with fear of loss, hope of gain,
love of life and pride in self
as we chase the Dunya
and strive for wealth.

Just name your pain, your passion,
your main vein of satisfaction!
That is your distraction-
when you stand, when you bow,
when you fall to the ground,
when you read the pure speech of Allah
while remembering everything else
except for Allah

We have to put aside this world
when we come to the prayer.
Don't worry about the worries
they will be there later.
Don't worry about your friends,
don't worry about the haters.
Don't worry about anything-
ALLAH IS GREATER!!

Don't worry about your work,
Don't worry about your weight,
Don't worry about the hurt,
don't worry about the hate
Don't worry about your watch-
it's never too late!
Just worry about Allah
and He will set things straight
As long as we pray straight
As long as we prostrate
As long as we show faith
As long as we know that-
there is no better place
Than in the company of Allah
because Allah is The Most Great

# ALLAHU AKBAR!!

وَاسْتَعِينُوا بِالصَّبْرِ وَالصَّلَاةِ

Seek assistance with patience and prayer

وَإِنَّهَا لَكَبِيرَةٌ إِلَّا عَلَى الْخَاشِعِين

And indeed it is heavy except upon who the
devout

[QURAN 2 : 45]

# THE PROMISE OF VICTORY

I am the promise of victory!
I am the promise of victory!
I am the promise!
I am the promise!
I am the promise of victory!

-Waiting to be claimed
Break me from these chains!
Nearly two billion believers
waiting for my reign
Praying to the All-Mighty
to take away my pains!

Everyday I complain to Allah
about my nation being slain
like The Children of Israel-
when their sons were being killed
And their women were defamed

And we the believers
bare the burden of blame
For if we did not transgress-
we would've never been shamed.

If we don't change
the condition in our self
then our condition will never change
And only through righteous action
can victory be gained...

So who wanna raise my flag
and stop waving it half mass?
Who's got enough faith
to face the aftermath?
Where are the heroes of the past-
ready to carry out the task?
Where is the brother of Harun-
with his staff?
When will Allah open up another path?

If I could perform miracles
*BY THE PEN* in my grasp...
I would strike the Red Sea
and try to split it in half!

I am the promise!
I am the promise!
I am the promise of victory!

Already written but yet to be read-
Not the path that you tread -
but the destination ahead.
Sacrifice is my oath
and faith is my pledge
Never let the degradation
replace the dedication in my legs

Whether trapped in the dark
or facing the ledge
Never let the devastation
take me to the edge
Inspiration instead.
It's just the way that I'm bred
Success in the flesh
until the day that I'm dead!

I am the promise!
I am the promise!
I am the promise of victory!

-Forgotten with history,
Because generation after generation
my nation lost identity
Too many prayers taken off
and it cost us mentally

Hardship. Misery.

How harsh is the penalty?

Allah took away fear

from the hearts of the enemy

Now the reign of Islam

is hardly a memory


But I've been trying to find my way back

into the hearts of the believers

Trying to find a way to reach out

to the scholars and the teachers

Trying to make the people see

that all of us are leaders

You're a shepherd and you know it man

It's all in your demeanor!


And maybe it's me,

but sometimes I look at this nation-

torn down to the ground

by the trials and tribulations

and I smile in admiration

because even though we went down

in humiliation

we stand back up

with marks of prostration!

The struggle making us stronger
It woke us up from our slumber
We were under the spell of the Dunya
and getting ready to wander

Now we prepare for victory
with humility and hunger
with the days of Ramadan
in the middle of the summer

And when the winter time comes
and the fast is light
we seek Allah's help
by standing at night

I am the promise of victory!
I am the promise of victory!
I am the promise!
I am the promise!
I am promise of victory!
In the land of the oppressed-
and only Allah can deliver me...

I AM THE PROMISE OF VICTORY!!

أَمْ حَسِبْتُمْ أَن تَدْخُلُوا الْجَنَّةَ وَلَمَّا يَأْتِكُم مَّثَلُ الَّذِينَ خَلَوْا مِن
قَبْلِكُم مَّسَّتْهُمُ الْبَأْسَاءُ وَالضَّرَّاءُ وَزُلْزِلُوا حَتَّىٰ يَقُولَ الرَّسُولُ
وَالَّذِينَ آمَنُوا مَعَهُ مَتَىٰ نَصْرُ اللَّهِ أَلَا إِنَّ نَصْرَ اللَّهِ قَرِيبٌ

Do you think that you will enter Paradise without
having suffered like those who passed away before
you? Affliction and hardship befell them and so
shaken were they that the Messenger and the
believers with him would exclaim: when comes the
victory of Allah? Surely the victory of Allah is near.

[QURAN 2 : 214]

# RAPTISM

This hip-hop blasphemy
got me ready to intervene
So somebody tell these rappers
It's time to come clean
It's bout to be the sequel-
The Story of Ibrahim
And these American Idols-
I'm bout to crush them with the Deen

The people blind following
They put their trust in the heartless
But Eminem is not a deity
he's nothing but an artist
They can all make claims
but what can they promise
And the message they proclaim
is turning us godless

Yet we prefer songs before The Psalms
and gossip before The Gospels-
conjecture before Quran
We've submitted ourselves
to the scripture of man

And accepted popular culture
over The Religion of Islam

I mean if it ain't got a kick and a snare
and some real dope drums
Enough bass in the headphones
to make your ears go numb
make the crowd go wild
and your peers go dumb
They say hip hop music
is the scripture of the slums

Mixing up the young,
until they're mentally undone
being taught by celebrities
that killing is fun
Until they're putting down the pencil
and they're picking up the gun
And the more the people listen-
the sicker they become

Lost in the phonics
of a philosophers logic
Quoting rappers all day
but won't acknowledge the Prophets

But who was it that parted the sea?
Who was it that healed the sick?
Who was it that split the moon?
Who was it that built the ship?

Real miracles by real men
by the permission of The Creator
The Prophet delivered the truth
without a pencil and paper
No mistakes, no eraser,
so who's ability is greater?
Thus, Allah challenges us
to bring something similar in nature

فَإِن لَّمْ تَفْعَلُوا وَلَن تَفْعَلُوا   Quran 2 : 24
For it is something that no man
has the ability to do
See, word play is no substitute
for real life parables
And making it rain with money
is not a real miracle

So is it Jeezy or Jesus
Jay Z or Joseph
Eminem or Muhammad
50 Cent or Moses?

Divinely inspired men
or rambling poets-
who only speak of desire
I mean haven't you noticed?

And I know it's hard to tell the truth
in a room full of liars
So most people don't sing
they just move with the choir
We're willing to accept
whatever suits our desires
but nobody in this world
is too cool for the fire

You think money can buy you bliss-
and fame is a blessing
but the success of this world
doesn't guarantee you heaven
You can't ransom your soul
with silver and gold
and you can go platinum and diamond
it won't lessen the load

Once them flames cover your face
and you're chained by the collar

and you can hear the horror
behind all the screams and the hollers
you won't care about your image,
you won't care about a dollar
you won't care about no rappers,
you won't care who's hotter

A thousand authors of lies
searching for validity
but won't read the Quran
or consider it's authenticity
There's a scarcity of sincerity
when it comes to the industry
because most lack the ability
to practice humility

Trapped in this track list
of backward mobility
where status depends
on how bad is your imagery
These rappers are all sick
and Islam is the remedy
yet they rather it be rap
that they practice religiously...

أَفَرَأَيْتَ مَنِ اتَّخَذَ إِلَهَهُ هَوَاهُ وَأَضَلَّهُ اللهُ عَلَى عِلْمٍ وَخَتَمَ عَلَى سَمْعِهِ
وَقَلْبِهِ وَجَعَلَ عَلَى بَصَرِهِ غِشَاوَةً فَمَن يَهْدِيهِ مِن بَعْدِ اللهِ أَفَلَا تَذَكَّرُونَ

Have you seen the one who took his desires as his
god, and Allah led him astray, despite his
knowledge, and He sealed his hearing and his
heart, and He made a veil on his eyes Who then
can guide him after Allah. Will you not take heed.

[QURAN 45 : 23]

# HOW COULD YOU SLEEP?

*Dreams don't happen when your eyes are closed*
*No paradise for blinded souls...*

Do we realize the beauty, the bounty,
the blessings of Islam?
Have we tasted the flavor, the favor,
the sweetness of Iman?

IF ONLY WE KNEW...
We'd sell ourselves
in the life of this world
for the price of the hereafter
IF ONLY WE KNEW...
We'd put an end to this book of sins
and start writing a new chapter

WAKE UP! To The Greatness,
The Honor, The Power of Allah
WAKE UP!  To the proof, embrace the truth
cause the hour isn't far

Too long we've been stuck in a slumber- SLEEP!
Some of our brothers and sisters are-IN TOO DEEP

Our youth are trapped
in the matrix of movies & music
Video games got them chained by the brain
Under the influence of pop culture-
dreaming of fame
This mainstream mentality is virtual reality

COME BACK! To the real world
where bombs drop on the lands of our brothers
COME BACK! To the real world
where babies die in the hands of our mothers

How Could You Sleep!?
When your heart is so far apart from this creed
How Could You Sleep!?
When we haven't begin to establish Tawheed
How Could You Sleep!?
When there's another hungry person to feed
How Could You Sleep!?
When you're the missing
link that this Ummah might need

This Ummah is in for a rude awakening. Vacationing.
Consumed in too much play station
and not enough Deen

This Dunya got us on a string
like puppets corrupted by material things
We call ourselves muslims
but don't remember what it means

We keep earphones screaming
to drown out the sound of believers bleeding
And how much blood has been shed
in the name of freedom
Our brothers and sisters
are being detained without reason
and yet we can't wait for the next NBA season

From Kobe & Lebron
to what's your favorite sitcom?
Anything to forget
about Muslims getting spit on
Long nights under the drone strikes
When reality hits home
It won't matter which of these rappers
just manufactured a hit song
Hiding our faces from the hatred
while they try to take away the sacred
They got us running for cover
like a baby without a blanket

How Could You Sleep!?
When your heart is so far apart from this creed
How Could You Sleep!?
When we haven't begin to establish Tawheed
How Could You Sleep!?
When there's another hungry person to feed
How Could You Sleep!?
When you're the missing link
that this Ummah might need

Under dressed to impress
everybody but the one worthy of praise
Material slaves.
Selling our souls at minimum wage
while history fades in the dwindling shade
of liberties grave

Freedom is what we claim in this land-
even though we've been chained by the hands,
by the cuffs of the shirt
and the name of the brand
We worship the creation of man

But real freedom is The Deen of Islam
Freedom to be as He commands

Freedom to bow and to stand
no matter where it is I am
To pray to Allah and to read His Quran

IF ONLY WE KNEW...
We'd free ourselves and our families
from the love of this Dunya,
wipe the sleep out of our eyes
and hold onto The Sunnah
IF ONLY WE KNEW...
We would laugh a little less
and let tears shed for The Ummah,
let go of right now and prepare for the future

How Could You Sleep!?
When your heart is so far apart from this creed
How Could You Sleep!?
When we haven't begin to establish Tawheed
How Could You Sleep!?
When there's another hungry person to feed
How Could You Sleep!?
When you're the missing link
that this Ummah might need

تَتَجَافَىٰ جُنُوبُهُمْ عَنِ الْمَضَاجِعِ يَدْعُونَ رَبَّهُمْ خَوْفًا وَطَمَعًا وَمِمَّا رَزَقْنَاهُمْ يُنفِقُونَ

Their sides forsake their beds, and they call upon their Lord in fear and in hope, and they are active in spending out of what we have provided them.

[Quran 32 : 16]

# VERSES THE WORLD

Flipping through the pages of the scripture
trying to find my place
in the bigger picture- I figure...
If revelation is meant
to guide man to his purpose
then my destiny must be written
in one of Allah's verses
And so I'm nervous-
from a punishment that's so severe
But steady treading a thin line
between hope and fear
because though the road is straight-
no man ever really knows his fate,
nor the load that his soul can take-
before he's left with a broken slate
And many do deeds
that'll hold no weight
cased closed on your soul
and there's no escape
I just pray I get through
before they close the gates
and I'm chosen to sit amongst those
who Allah shows His Face!

For The Pharaohs that I loathe
and the stones that I break
For The Prophets that I love
and their foes that I hate
For the orphans that I clothe
and the cold they escape
For the poor and the hungry
and the old and the late
For every person that I know
with a soul full of faith
For the heads that are bowed
and the rows that are straight
For the sake of Allah
and I long for His Grace
For only in His Word
does my soul feel safe
And when I read-
I see much more than just creed
it's more like living a life-
written with Tajweed
Every breath is a sign
so remember to take heed
The Quran is alive
this ain't make believe
And you can give them the truth
but can't make them believe

Oppression in the ink
making the pages bleed
Put the rage in the cage
or the hatred breeds
Transgression on the brink-
looking for a place to feed
but the hunger of the fast
overtakes the greed
Another verse come to pass
another fate decreed
Another hearse on the way
another family grieves
The hardship precedes
then comes the ease
but people forget Allah
when the tribulation leaves
And its back to The Dunya
when the pains relieved
The afterlife is a reality
we can't conceive
Temporary is this world
but man is deceived
What you send forth from this life
is what your hands receive
So wear His commands like cuffs
until your hands are freed

And as for me...
I could be anywhere in the book-
seeing the signs of Allah
everywhere that I look
every chapter, every Ayah,
every line that He put
History repeats man-
I'm living in the time of Lut
Noah and his people,
Ibrahim and Namrut
and tomorrow I could be Yunus
in the belly of The Hute
Or taking on a tyrant-
David and Goliath
I'm the stone that was thrown
to take down a giant
The road that I'm following-
both old and modern
unrolls like scrolls
and leads to the throne of Solomon
Behold! In my hold
is the sword of an Ottoman
Poet by trade
but there's a warrior inside of him

Laughing at these sorcerers-
people won't behave
So I might disappear
like The People of The Cave
Getting deeper in the page,
but I'm trying to stay afloat
Am I the boat that was scuttled,
or the scuttle in the boat?
The boy that was killed
or the wall rebuilt?
The treasure underneath it,
or the people in the town
that was destined to keep it?
Is a king on my course
taken ships by force
And Gog and Magog
still oppressing the poor?
Where's Dhul-Qarnain
and the rest of them boys?
Can't you see the whole world
is infested with wars?
Gotta listen real close
to hear The Messenger's voice
Saying "Victory Is Written"
so let the believers rejoice!

وَيُرِيكُمْ آيَاتِهِ فَأَيَّ آيَاتِ اللهِ تُنكِرُونَ

And He (Allah) shows you His signs and wonders
Then which of Allah's signs will you deny?

[Quran 40 : 81]

# MOTHERS OF THE BELIEVERS

Imagine if you were Hajjar...
Running back and forth
between Saffa and Marwa
in the hottest place on the earth-
searching for water
Imagine your son dying of thirst
in the absence of his father
Just to save his life- what would you offer?
Would you hold on to your faith
or would you falter
Before he ever gets the chance
to help his father build the Ka'ba
Before he ever sees the day
that he agrees to be slaughtered
I wonder in our weakness-
how many dreams that we've altered

Now imagine the army of Pharaoh
as it slowly approaches
Time is running short
and you're the mother of Moses
You hear a knock at the door
and for a moment you're hopeless
afraid for your child and unable to focus

Would you give in to the pressure
and willingly surrender
or would you put your trust in Allah
and put the baby in the river?
What if you give him to a tyrant
and he never parted the Sea
and he never lives to see the day
that he would set you free
And we know everything happens
by Allah's decree
but if we don't do the right things
then where would we be?

So many young men
with their futures unwritten
and what would they become
without dedicated women
I've seen so many die
without ever really living
So I gotta thank my mother
for everything she's given

The sacrifices that she made
just to carry on tradition
but The Zam Zam she gave
wasn't water it was wisdom

50

See, I too was born in a time
when they were burying their children
given to society then buried in the system

So many Yusuf's that never had a vision
So many Ibrahim's that never had dreams
He could've been Musa raised amongst kings
or maybe Ismail made to burst springs

So many young women
with the potential of Mary
give it up in a hurry
and give up on getting married
Could've been Khadijah,
Mother of The Believers
but it takes a strong woman
to raise up a leader

We need more Fatimas, we need more Aishas,
we need more Zaynabs, we need more Aasiyas
Sumayyah, Ruqayyah- women of prayer
Before you start mimicking other women
you should remember Nusaibah
not willing to waiver - and not many were braver
And when Asmaa was nearly in labor-
she would still walk five miles to deliver the favor

Remember what they gave
without any ambition of getting paid
So men like me could be saved
and raised up to give praise
and behave like a grateful slave
So when women enter the premises
then lower your gaze!

And as for the one who was made
from my rib cage-
I wage war until her tears fade
trying to balance the world
on her shoulder blades
You gotta follow the steps
down that road they paved
cause every time you raise a soldier
more souls get saved
I said every time you raise a soldier
more souls get saved

And we could never repay you
for what you carry in your wombs
I mean- how could we ever build an Ummah
if we never had an Umm!
How could we ever build an Ummah
if we never had an Umm!

إِذْ قَالَتِ امْرَأَتُ عِمْرَانَ رَبِّ إِنِّي نَذَرْتُ لَكَ مَا فِي
بَطْنِي مُحَرَّرًا فَتَقَبَّلْ مِنِّي إِنَّكَ أَنتَ السَّمِيعُ الْعَلِيمُ

When the woman of Imran said:
"My Lord! Indeed I vow to you that the child in my womb
is to be devoted to Your exclusive service.
So then accept that from me.
Surely You alone are All-Hearing, All-Knowing."

[Quran 3 : 35]

# YOU WILL BE ALONE

I don't know of any moment as lonely
as being lowered into the grave
except for the day that your soul will be raised
not knowing where you're going
you can only be afraid

I only hope that you prayed,
I only hope that you gave,
I only hope that you lived
as an obedient slave,
I hope you repented
for the mistakes that you made,
 And as for those who wronged you-
I hope you forgave!

We don't know our own fate
we only hope to be saved-
from the blaze of the fire,
better tame your desires
so regret will not chase you
on the day you expire

Because you will be alone-
once they bury your bones

your wealth and your family
will go back home
The only thing you really own are your deeds
still by your side when everybody leaves

Whatever you did in this life
whether righteous or wretched
Will be your companion
until the time you're resurrected

We don't like to think about death
until we're one foot in the ground
and this world has let us down
and everything we loved
is nowhere to be found
and the only thing that matters now
is where are we bound?

Did you know that everyone of us
will be put on trial
whether we put on a suit or put on a shroud
Those two angels will visit us in the grave
and question our knowledge like-
Who was your Lord?
What was your religion?
And who was your Prophet?

And only the truthful will respond
with truth on that day
but the liars won't even know what to say
and the burden will be so heavy,
and the moment will be so scary
that no one would want to carry that load
A man might give up his wealth
and his family just to ransom his soul
from a fire whose fuel is men and stone

I don't know of any moment as lonely
as being lowered into the grave
except for the day that your soul will be raised
not knowing where you're going
you can only be afraid

We were told to often remember death
and that life is just a test
whereby Allah makes it known
whose conduct is best
In this conquest to conquer the flesh-
we have to constantly reflect
on the blessings bestowed
that we so often forget

Knee deep in neglect-
why do we leave off Allah until later?
when we should be constant in prayer
in dread of the day
when we stand before The Creator
and He ask His servants:
What have you done with My Favors?

I only hope that you prayed,
I only hope that you gave,
I only hope that you lived
as an obedient slave,
I hope you repented
for the mistakes that you made,
and as for those who wronged you-
I hope you forgave!

We will be alone
when we are lowered into the grave
and we don't know our own fate
We only hope to be saved.

يَوْمَ يَفِرُّ الْمَرْءُ مِنْ أَخِيهِ وَأُمِّهِ وَأَبِيهِ وَصَاحِبَتِهِ وَبَنِيهِ

لِكُلِّ امْرِئٍ مِنْهُمْ يَوْمَئِذٍ شَأْنٌ يُغْنِيهِ

A day when a person runs from his brother and his mother and his father and his companions and his children. For every person that day there is enough concerns of his own to occupy him completely.

[Quran 80 : 33-37]

# THE HOUR IS NEAR

When the blessing is taken out of time
and it goes faster and faster
When earthquakes increase
and natural disasters
When the weather becomes extreme
When Arabia turns green
When barefooted bedouins compete
in building buildings to the sky
like Saudi, Abu Dhabi, Bahrain and Dubai

When literacy increases
but knowledge is lost
When the believers will be many
but weaker than froth
When false prophets appear-
know that the hour is near
though sometimes I get the feeling
that it's already here...

The Last Prophet sent to mankind
told us about the signs
that will happen on earth
before the ending of time

When music is widespread
and people wear it on their heads
When children are filled with rage
When the wife is respected
and the mother is disobeyed

When the pious will disappear
and trust will decrease
When people are intimate in public streets
When women will be dressed
but appear to be naked
When the institution of marriage
is no longer sacred

When the liar is believed
and the people are deceived
and the worst of the worst are chosen to lead
When the number of police begin to increase
When trials begin to appear in the east

When all the nations will gather
against the believers
See the hour has a face
and these are it's features

When the one who is killed
doesn't know the reason they had to die
and even the killer himself
doesn't even know why

When nothing of Islam
remains except for the names
and people abandon the religion
for a worldly gain

When there is war between Muslims and Jews
When the speakers will be many
but the scholars will be few

When the followers of Muhammad
will be setting up rivals
praying to graves and worshipping idols
When people gather for congregation
and no one prays with concentration

When the mosque will be lovely
but the hearts will be ugly
and lives will be ruined
in the conquest for money

When interest will increase
and there is so much credit and debt
that no one would be able to avoid its effects

The signs are so clear - That the hour is near
But sometimes I get the feeling
that it's already here

When no one is able to make the Hajj-
to visit the ancient mosque
When the believer wakes up
and his faith has been lost

When the Anti-Christ appears-
that one eyed beast
When Gog and Magog
come out from The East
When Jesus descends from the skies
dripping of pearls
Then you know we have approached
the end of this world

When the sun rises from the west
and the pen has been lifted
there will be no repentance
if you haven't submitted

These are not just events
that The Prophet predicted
because prophecies are promises
that are already scripted

The Last Prophet sent to mankind
told us about the signs
that will happen on earth
before the ending of time

The first will be his death
when he breathes his last breath
and it's been over 1400 years since
he was laid to rest
But before he left he told us about the end
what was written BY THE PEN
He told us about Iraq
where the trials will begin
And we are living in the last days,
holding on to hot coals,
doing our best not to lose our souls

The minor signs have appeared
and the hour is near
But sometimes I get the feeling
that it's already here

يَسْـأَلُونَكَ عَنِ السَّاعَةِ أَيَّانَ مُرْسَاهَا

قُلْ إِنَّمَا عِلْمُهَا عِندَ رَبِّي

They ask you about The Hour

Say the knowledge of it belongs to my Lord alone!

[Quran 7 : 187]

# IF I DO NOT WRITE

The pen has been lifted
and the ink has dried
and what happens tomorrow
is not for me to decide...
I am only a scribe,
using my pen to survive
For if I do not write
then my spirit has died
For if I do not right-
I'm not even alive

I was taught to do right
that's the reason I strive-
that's the reason I thrive-
that's the reason I rise
and reach for the sky-
like a kid from the bottom
that still believes he can fly

If I do not right
I might bleed from the eyes-
with the pain of an Ummah
etched deep inside

I'm buried alive
between people and pride
and every time I do write
 it's like I'm being revived

And if I do not write
then my spirit has died
And if I do not right
I'm not even alive.

What are the rights of a scribe?
With a life full of strife
he either writes or he cries,
he dies for the truth
before he fights for the lies

His words are advice to the wise
His verses like sight to the blind
This is light for the mind
If I do not write then I do not shine

This is not just rhyme –
this is my life on the line
because I don't write just to write
but to fight against crime

If I do not right
then I have wronged my soul-
and neglected my duty
to humanity as a whole
I must do write
for the rights I uphold
For their plights are untold
For the life that gets sold
at the price of fools gold

And you can say what you like
but no pen in the world
could ever make that right
That's why I take it to the page-
late into the night
then take it to the stage-
and say it on the mic
What good are my words
if I'm afraid to recite?
For a scribe is not a scribe
unless he makes things right

The pen has been lifted
and the ink has dried
My blood has been tested
and there is ink inside

And if I do not write
then my spirit has died
And if I do not right
I'm not even alive.
I am only a scribe
using my pen to survive
and what happens tomorrow
is not for me to decide

I have no rights to the future-
my only portion of fate-
is that I write my own history
with the choices I make
I've got the choice to be great
or the choice to be late
and if I don't choose right
my destruction awaits

See, I could be the author of hate
but rather I illustrate peace-
to eliminate grief
and penetrate the hearts
with the rhythm of speech
The life of a poet is the dripping of ink-
and when it dries -
I must write to survive

It's just the life of a scribe
For if I do not write
then my spirit has died
And if I do not right
I'm not even alive

If I don't do right
I might bleed from the eyes-
with the pain of an Ummah
etched deep inside
I'm buried alive
between people and pride
and every time I do right
it's like I'm being revived.

وَالْعَصْرِ - إِنَّ الْإِنسَانَ لَفِي خُسْرٍ

إِلَّا الَّذِينَ آمَنُوا وَعَمِلُوا الصَّالِحَاتِ

وَتَوَاصَوْا بِالْحَقِّ وَتَوَاصَوْا بِالصَّبْرِ

By The Time, Mankind is in a state of loss,
Except those who believe and act righteously
And enjoin one another by truth
And enjoin one another by patience.

[Quran 103 : 1-3]

# GLOSSARY

**Allah** : Arabic Name of The One & Only True God
**Allahu Akbar** : Allah is The Greatest
**Ameen** : After Supplication Muslims Say Ameen!
**Athan** : Muslim Call to Prayer
**Ayah** : Refers to Signs, Verses or Proofs of Allah
**Deen** : Religion or System of Life
**Dhul-Qarnain** : A Righteous Ruler Mentioned In The Quran
**Dunya** : Temporary Worldly Life
**Fajr** : Dawn Prayer
**Fitnah** : Temptation or Trial
**Gog & Magog** : A Wretched People From The Offspring of Adam
**Hajj** : Sacred Pilgrimage To Mecca
**Hajjar** : Wife of Abraham and Mother of Ishmael
**Haroon** : Arabic for Aaron the Brother of The Prophet Moses
**Hute** : Giant Whale
**Ibrahim** : Arabic for Abraham
**Iqama** : Shortened or Immediate Call To Prayer
**Islam** : Submission To Allah (The Religion of All The Prophets)
**Ka'ba** : The Sacred House In Mecca
**Lut** : Arabic for Lot, A Prophet of Allah
**Marwa** : A Small Mountain In Mecca
**Musa** : Arabic for Moses A Prophet of Allah
**Muslim** : One Who Submits to Allah and Follows Islam
**Namrut** : Arabic for Nimrod a Tyrant During The Time of Abraham
**Noor** : Light
**Ramadan** : Month of Fasting For Muslims
**Saffa** : A Small Mountain In Mecca
**Sahaba** : Companions or Disciples of The Prophet Muhammad
**Salaam** : Greeting of Peace
**Sunnah** : The Traditions of The Prophet Muhammad
**Tajweed** : The Science of Reciting The Quran
**Takbeer** : To Proclaim Allah's Greatness
**Tawheed** : The Oneness of Allah (Pure Monotheism)
**Umm** : Mother
**Ummah** : Community or Nation
**Qibla** : Direction of Prayer
**Quran** : The Last & Final Revelation Sent To Mankind
**Yusuf** : Arabic for Joseph, A Prophet of Allah

E: gijaaber@gmail.com

www.gijaaber.com
www.facebook.com/gijaaber
www.youtube.com/gijaaber

To Zunaira

I really appreciate your support.
May Allah grant you success in
everything you do. Ameen!